We Don't Know That This Is Temporary

by Adrienne Marie Barrios

STANCHION

Published by Stanchion Books, LLC
StanchionZine.com
Cover art by Jeff Bogle
ISBN: 979-8-89292-683-6

We Don't Know That This Is Temporary

by Adrienne Marie Barrios

STANCHION

for my favorite poet,
wherever she may be

These poems deal with graphic physical and mental health issues. Please read with care.

"I was telling someone not long ago how I for years had the persistent feeling inside me that I missed someone, longed to be with them again, and for years, I searched out there for them, and only after one of those strange dreams where you have emotional bombs, in this dream, I almost remembered my real name, and when I woke, I realized the person I mourned and missed was myself."

—Micah Chaim Thomas,
author of the *Eudaimonia* series

Prologue

"Leigh Chadwick"

I learned that people are obsessed with learning. I learned that I have to eat bacon and cheese for breakfast, or I might forget the love I used to feel when a stranger's eye caught mine as I crossed Winchester on a morning walk. Well, not love. I learned that love might not be real. I learned that even if I say certain words, I might only mean them as much as my cat who rubs against my leg after forgetting it already ate two breakfasts. I learned that I can go 618 days without seeing my family and only just start to miss them. I learned that wheat, onions, beans, apples, nectarines, garlic, and dairy make me sick, and that 4,725,899 people can die and someone will still call it a hoax. I learned that I am autistic. I learned that I want more. I learned the lie of an evening and how long it takes for my desires to become my desires. I learned that feelings come and go. Like fathers. Like love. Like 617 empty days.

I

"Firsts"

A twin bed tucked inside a closet, a hot pink room at the end of a
hall. Your ecstasy overflows, and I think, *Is this it?*

Late-night phone calls, dreaming Paris,
green velveteen cushions, a piano on hardwood floors
in an attic apartment, a bed with no frame. Time is a movie
running backward down the street lined with dogwood trees.
A nickname given because of you, *little dick fucker*,
a secret taunt of one who doesn't know: sometimes less is more.

A tryst of understanding,
your memory twists and frays, a Message given,
I am not good for you—so They say—I am not good for you.
Your soul in the balance.

We don't know that this is temporary.

Still a child, roaming with my friends, summer budding from our
eyes, and then, you, curly hair and capricious grin, and your
hand takes my heart.

A betrayal, and
my memory twists and shames, a Message received,
I am not good for Him—so They say—*You are not good; repent.*

None of this is temporary.

A phone call of a different sort, standing on the curb, life pans
around me. You sob, and I can't
hear your voice above the music.

We don't know that this is temporary.

"Practice"

You, a knee between my legs,
me, a tongue colliding—
we were practicing, but for what?

You disappeared. I married the opposite of
femininity, bones and rough edges, and you
became an anecdote, a memory, a fragment of shame.

"Juniper Seeds"

Pine makes
a tenuous home
in my mouth and
you, above, aloof,
move inside me, but
I wonder, *How did we get
here?* from where we stood
before, and you ask me, *Where
do you want it?* but the question evades
the forest growing from my throat, and I am
lost in the trees and the weeds planted years ago,
hazy, unaware of the flower we might be planting now.

"Satisfaction"

I never think of you during sex, but
sometimes, I think about you after,
about that time we balanced
against the far end of my makeshift wooden loft.
You thought you held me up as I
straddled the narrow, pale width of your lap
bearing most of the weight myself.
You came inside me, gasping,
and as you said,
Wow, that was incredible, wasn't it? I thought,
Am I invisible to you?

I think about how I don't remember any orgasms with you
except yours;
the way you would climax and pass out still inside me,
already smelling as if you'd slept for ten hours.

I think about the first time, the way
I pushed up toward you, wanting to kiss you more, and
you pulled back,
Whoa, there, smirking,
my passion a joke.
You helped me out of my clothes,
put two fingers inside me, felt the hard plastic
ring, and said,
Are we good?

I think about that time toward the end,
days after you punched the couch just an inch to my right,
when you looked at me
across our one-bedroom apartment and screamed,
It's like you're saying I'm not satisfying you.
You weren't.

I think about the flight home from San Francisco,
in the beginning,
a spontaneous trip to see Damien Rice,
and you watched me weep at the
beauty of his voice
reverberating off synagogue walls,
his visceral emotion,
unhampered by dissatisfaction,
enhanced by it.
I think about the lust on that plane,
hands barely able to stop
touching, heavy breath,
flushed cheeks.
I think about
the rushed sex of
I promised them I'd be there.

How quickly things dissipate.

"Leigh Chadwick Pt. 2"

I learned that time does not heal all wounds. I learned that the
way you look at me makes me wish you wouldn't, because
what's the point of eyes that do not see? I learned that my heart
didn't form properly, a whole gaping between two parts that wilt
like unwatered flowers, faltering as bubbles dance and flutter. I
learned that learning doesn't really solve much and that proper
medication can make me see the light that pierces the shadows
on a Monday morning instead of the dust hovering above the
ground. I learned that I would like to learn how a person
becomes a friend, how a wife becomes a better wife. I learned to
make a Provençal—2 oz. lavender gin, 1 ¼ oz. Vermouth de
Provence vermouth, ¾ oz. Cointreau, orange twist. I learned how
to make lavender gin and Vermouth de Provence, and that
drinking a 4 oz. martini on an empty stomach heals many
wounds, and when you boil lavender with gin, it turns blue, and I
could lose myself in a pot of blue for days. I learned that I can
bleed from just about anywhere. All I have to do is try.

"If You Wanted"

If you had wanted me to stay,
you should have told me
that I looked nice.
When you fucked me,
you should have
held my face in your hands,
touched my palms with the tips
of your fingers, or run your hand
softly down the length of my arm.

You could have said I looked
pretty or
sexy or
something, anything other than
I don't think about your weight, or
I don't like it when you match.

If you really wanted me to stay, when I asked you,
Why are you married to me?
you could have said
something more
         than *I don't know.*

"Longing"

I hear the silverware clack as you put it away in the other room,
your extra chores attempts to bridge the divide that grows
between us, and I wonder:
do deep connections exist,
or is this a lie the movies tell us?
Will my soul ever ache for another person, or will it ache forever
for the absence of one, the space they could have filled
      if they had made themselves known to me?

"The Girl of Fruit Stand #428"

And does her husband know
that when she sees her, butterflies
twitch
like a school-girl crush, the way her smile
pulls at the corners of her mouth,
just slightly, the way her slight frame holds
so much beauty. Does her husband know
that she can't keep her heart from
longing
for the knowledge of her touch?

"Leigh Chadwick Pt. 3"

I unlearned the idea that lithium could make me constantly happy—what is happy, anyway?— and that it doesn't make you gain weight—it just makes you thirsty, and it's about what you use to quench. None of this is true. I unlearned my proclivity for sweets—this isn't true, either—but not soon enough, because teeth can't unlearn their cavities. I unlearned how to sleep in on a Saturday morning when the cats are hungry and I have no other need to wake. There's always a need when time is short. Time is always short. I unlearned my aversion to being alone, if pretending is unlearning and Xanax is amnesia. I unlearned the way my mind drifts to you each day at unexpected times, at all times, at times when I start to think *Maybe it won't*. I unlearned the lie of the evening and the unreliability of my feelings, because feelings aren't real. We have only decisions. I unlearned my annoyance for cats. They only want to be cared for, touched, fed, noticed, brushed, rubbed, held, scratched, snuggled, loved, coddled, held, held. Held. Held. They only want what I want.

"Featherbones"

When he's gone, I sing about the desert sky, the way you woke in the morning to find her gone, the space where she slept now yours. When he's gone, I sing about the woman who broke your heart, fast and deep—the woman whose painting you kept in our bedroom, an unformed question I took years to ask. When he's gone, I remember the night we sang it together, the crowded bar so quiet we could hear the ice shift in the tin as vodka ran down the cubes, cracking, settling, the perfection we created, if only for some minutes, a blip in a string of nights, weeks not worth remembering. When he's gone, I sing your notes, your lines—I leave the hole I used to fill when we sang about her together, the imagined croon of your new lover filling mine.

"Poem"

What if
I never touched him again,
if the last time we touched was
one brush against his skin that
he tried to avoid,
an unwanted plea at the edge
of his rejection?
I know what they say.
They say,
You should never believe a cheater.
They say,
A cheater will never leave.
It's the years you can't replace.
But do you know how long it's been
since I've heard the words *I love you?*
Or the last time someone touched my face
or held my gaze
with more than indifference?

"Please, for the Love of God, Touch Me"

We dance around each other, day and night, our eyes not quite
meeting, our bodies opposing fields three miles thick. Requests
come by courier text from rooms away, delayed on the slow
current of unreliable Wi-Fi forced to travel through centuries-old
concrete and stale air just to reach my filthy phone from his.
Twin phones, bought new, yet so different. *Can you make me a
coffee?* The clicking—click click click clicking all day and all
night, the incessant click clicking of his mouse and mechanical
keyboard, the same game from dawn until dusk 'til his eyes grow
heavy and then the click clicking slows but never stops. *Are you
hungry?* Small words bend around corners into the thick foam-
covered silence of his room, dark reds and grays checkered floor
to ceiling absorbing sound as if they were designed to eliminate
—and they were, and they do. And is it really a question if I plan
to make dinner anyway? The silence breeds silence breeds
growth of the sounds in my ears until all I can hear is the
whoosh-whooshing of my own heart and my blood, just whoosh-
whooshing and thudding in my ears, so loud and so constant that
when he finally speaks, I can't hear what he says. *What?* He
doesn't repeat. I grow tired of pretending to be entertained by my
own hobbies that don't exist because what could I possibly want
more than him? *I'm going to bed.* Four rooms is an ocean of cat
fur and hot air, and my phone collects silence by my side of the
bed, the whoosh-whooshing my lullaby as the time between
peeks at my empty screen grows until it becomes infinite, and I
dream—*Your message could not be sent.*—of his fingers tracing
my back, running lightly up my arms and through my hair, of his
lips just below my ear, when words were sounds and phones
were mouths and the tundra of sheets between us couldn't keep
us from pressing our atoms together, together, as if trying so hard
might finally prove them wrong: We *can* touch! We can touch.
We can. *Please, for the love of God, touch me.*

II

II

"Revelation"

I miss
the scent of your skin that
I can't remember,
the way your hair twists
at certain spots
that I don't know,
the way you smile
at something cheeky—
a smile I've never seen.
I miss the years we've wasted
pretending to be happy
with other people.

"I Learned the Word Limerence This Week, but I Think a Part of Me Always Knew"

When the day ends and the attention with it, sure, I think of him. Of the way I wish he wanted what I want, of the closeness I know isn't real. Can't be real. And it isn't him that descends, with his words and his charms and alluring aloof glances. And sure, sometimes I think of you, of the easy way you'll give me attention any moment I demand—at my whim, you're there, enraptured by my very presence. But it isn't you, with your boyish smile and the way you could look at me for hours and never tire of my face. And it isn't him, with his distant stare and that mouth that can make me come any time I want. No—if I think of you, any of you, it is with desperation, a pleading wish for you to see me, really see me, down here, deep in this pit, the pit you claim as your home before you head out for the game, or the show, or the bar, the pit you leave behind but that I can never let go, the pit that takes joys and triumphs and loves and morphs them, changes them into lesser versions of themselves, or obsessions, never enough, never enough. When the day ends, the emptiness descends, and you, none of you, are anywhere at all.

"Hayden"

When I think of your name, it is a breath on my lips, a whisper, something not quite formed: *Hayden*. Your name is a promise I broke at least three times. Maybe I'll break it forever. Your name is an echo from your own throat when I tell you I've applied my lipstick three times now, four, and it's still not quite right. I can't keep my hand steady. *Deep breaths, darling.* Your name is the way I don't stop as I drive across the old Lake Sammamish bridge, keep driving when I see James and Colin fixing a tire on that old rusty car. James looks so frail, the wind might carry him, I might be able to hold him down. But I want to get to you more. Your name is matching purple funeral clothes in the parking lot behind the Issaquah Community Center, bones jutting from ribcages long before fat settled in, lines etched in a face dipped in the sorrow of Eric's death. Your name is a steady gaze around the bar where most of us drink too much, hoping to forget—a steady hand to hold me up. Your name is where I laid my body next to yours, where something was born, something of need that only loss can bring, the inevitable abdication of control, our lips pressing together in Jessica's bed as I breathe you in. *Does this feel good, darling?* Your name is the way you ask if it's okay as I shudder, whimper, your hand running up the inside of my thigh, sliding inside, an impossible truth, the words little more than a breath in my ear, a question for which you already know the answer.

"Perspective"

When you fuck him, do you think about me?
When he's inside you, do you wonder how
I might feel instead of him?
Do you wonder what it would be like
if I held your face between my palms,
your sight level with mine,
steady—
if I held your gaze for
one minute,
two minutes,
five minutes,
if your heart started to pound with the tension
forming between our eyes,
pupils dilated,
if your thoughts raced and then quieted
then raced again—
if your mouth fell open
just slightly
because the breath through your nose wasn't enough,
if your body moved closer to mine,
on instinct,
as if the space between closed with the years,
suddenly flattened through time,
and then,
when our lips finally met,
we breathed each other in,
colliding,
salt on tongues on cheeks,
the scenes we've dreamed,
finally realized?

"If I say I love you right now, will you hold it against me? Because I've lost a lot of blood."

What if, when I said your name, it wasn't a lie anymore? What if it spilled through the cracks in my marigold Anthropologie curtains and wove between the particles of dust and dissipated into the air like clove and orange oil room mist, but less heavy and more resilient? What if, when I said your name, it came with a touch, your hand at the nape of my neck where the hair dye never seems to reach, your lips hungry against my shoulder? What if your name meant *goldenrod* and *gleaming* and *magnificence*, and your lip print melted into my skin like an invisible tattoo? What if, when I said your name, you said mine, and we pretended, for a moment, it had always been that way?

"Three Years"

I didn't expect three years and three thousand miles to evaporate in an instant. I didn't expect the air to feel like teeth through blueberries in summer's first pie or the smell of rain on an afternoon that waffles between *Should we go to Bathtub Gin* and *I wish you could climb under these covers and remind me that I'm real.* I didn't expect steak to become an honesty that I didn't realize I'd left on California Ave, or that trees the colors of Issaquah High School and longing lining the streets would make my heart want to shatter into smaller hearts that I might sprinkle on each corner of this city so that my heart is here with you. I didn't expect leaving to feel like tearing muscle from bone, like pulling one fiber from my body with each step I took. I didn't expect that a place once filled with *you know I can't live here anymore* and *why didn't you come forward to the police sooner* could become new again, whole again, warm again. I didn't expect to feel, so suddenly, like maybe I can, too.

"Do You Think That We Could Work Out a Sign"

My chest hurts, and I call it anxiety. My chest hurts, and I say it's heartburn from the third night in a row that we've eaten spaghetti because I can't figure out what else to make anymore. My chest hurts, and I say something like, *I just don't feel very well. No, I don't need anything. Yes, I'm sure.* My chest hurts, and all I can see is your face when you smile, and all I can smell is imagined skin after a shower, and all I can taste is the metallic fear on my tongue moments before saying goodbye to you for what I knew would be the last time. My chest hurts, and I take a Xanax. Then I take another. And then I take five more, and I stare at the wall, waiting for time to become something I can change.

"In Some Sacred Place"

Your name is a breath catching, tucked between *If I don't say this now, I will surely break* and *I'd give my body to be back again in the rest of the room.* Your name is air down the wrong pipe, stuck and painful between my ribs. Your name is the empty time I've forgotten how to fill and the burn of loneliness that I had become used to avoiding. Your name is a waking vision of purple and a wide-open grass lawn, of chairs lined in rows tied together with silk ribbons, of you, older, etched in time, your smile fastened unendingly to your boyish face, my hair swinging against lace in the light wind leading me to you. Your name is a lie that became truth, a truth I've given up, a truth that will never be mine.

"Aftermath"

Your name
becomes a
weapon used
to remind
me how
much *less*
I have
become.

"If I Was Watching You, What Were You Watching?"

Your eyes are etched with neglect, hardened with years of
acquired strength, dipped in loneliness you made for yourself,
and the way you don't look at me plants an ache deep inside me
every time, a tree that burns to ash the moment it starts to grow
because what can grow without hope, what can grow without
light and food and water, what can grow without a chance—what
can flourish when it isn't wanted, and if you don't want it, then
what are we still doing here?

"Dissociation"

Your name could be a memory I recount—if it felt like a
memory, not a dream. Your name is an illusion: the illusion of
comfort, of promises that can't be kept, of sugar that baits and
then tricks the mind into wanting more of a thing it shouldn't
have. Your name is the way I pretended to feel something that
wasn't real, a figment of my desire, but not for you. Your name
is the way the clouds look fake in the sky just before sunset in
winter, light gone too soon, bubbling soft edges and glossy sheen
like a video game I wish I'd never played. Your name is flashes
and glimpses, a nightmare I might slowly forget.

"When there's nothing left to burn / You have to set yourself on fire"

Your memory is coffee gone cold at ten o'clock in the morning, the sudden sting of panic when my body remembers what it has done as my mind refuses. Your memory is lingering iron, the palpitation lurching in my chest, skin pricking from the sudden rush of blood to my face.
Your memory—
      is it even real?—
           keeps me awake in the night,
              shutters my eyes in the day.

"Lithium"

Your name slips to the back of my mind where I keep words like *Terry, Westminster, possible restraining order, Mary,* a rippling that calms and smooths as you fall and fall and grow smaller with each moment. Your name catches an errant bubble, bobbing toward the surface, but I anchor you in place with words like *fabrication, integrity, ignorance, wife—Wife.* Your name becomes foreign, a sound my mouth forgets how to make, never knew how to make well. Your name slips into nothing, and in the place where you'd burrowed too deep, now gaping, new words bloom, words like *stay, decade, hold, pleasure, husband—Husband.* Your name gives way, and suddenly, again, with much more fullness, my heart remembers what it is to say *his* name.

"My Love"

His name is the swell in my chest as I wait for my chai to heat
and the shot of ginger and turmeric to burn down my throat and
into my heart because he's in the rest of the room; he's not far
behind me. His name is the structure to my days and the security
in my evenings. His name is the sound I make when I laugh so
hard I completely lose myself, in the way only joy can make real.
His name is the proof that, sometimes, if you're lucky, if you
want it badly enough and you keep your feet on the ground and
your heart in one piece, *I can't do this anymore* can come back
around to *This is all I've ever wanted. For ten years, this is all
I've ever wanted.*

III

"Wanting"

Wanting is not a momentary flash of desire. Wanting does not come and go in a flippant way, an easy way. Wanting inundates my mind, seeping in from every edge of thought or subtle pause. Wanting takes hold, erases what came before, and maybe after. Wanting is insatiable, a tongue that needs sour until it's raw and bleeding. An arm that needs pain until it's sore and bruised. An ear that needs that one song, on repeat, until sound is nothing but ringing and whooshing and mush. And even then, I want. Wanting is intangible. Wanting is irreplaceable, unescapable. I cannot be satisfied.

"Leigh Chadwick Pt. 10"

I learned that affection in the face of crisis quickly dissipates
when obligation and mundanity return—loneliness and untended
pain my most constant companions. I learned that a furry face
and tufted ears, biscuits made in sheets unchanged for weeks, a
wet nose buried in the palm of my hand can bring me to tears—
the reach of that nose for more as I turn away, the deep rumble of
a hand against a sleepy side. But I learned that this innocent need
only makes my own that much sharper: for his hand, your hand,
anyone's goddamn hand to touch my face, neck, arm, hair, face,
face, face—someone against whom I can bury my ever-cold nose
and know that I will always be safe.

"Affection"

I dream about pineapple, sweet and
soft against my tongue, tastebuds raised,
aroused, scraping flesh with flesh until my
hundredth, thousandth piece, straight
from the fridge, door open, supplied by puffy fingers,
lifts each tender bump, one by one by
one, gaping, raw and torn and
stinging, waiting for you to tell me to
stop.

"How to Write"

I don't know how to write a single thing when
your face appears on the street, appears in the screens on
bodies that aren't yours, sitting, smiling, arguing, fighting,
reminding me that it's been 301 days and some hours since
I told you, *I'm sorry, I can't, I didn't expect this*, and you said
something I never read.

I don't know how to write a single thing when
all I want is to tell you the things I've wanted to say since
301 days and some hours passed in silence, the lack of words
reminding me that our lives keep growing, changing, moving
forward, separately. I'm sorry; I didn't expect this—to say
you're someone I'll never forget.

"I wish things were better for you. For everyone."

I realize I don't know what better means anymore. Every choice has a negative, a consequence, two evils of which to be the lesser. I realize we're all trading on the least worst possible outcome, but never the best. The fewest bullet wounds, but never zero. The fewest entry points, but still fewer exits. How would I name a child never meant to live longer than the length of a breath exhaled to steady a hand? I realize I was never meant to answer that question, and I pack my uterus in a box and bury it beneath the tree that makes me sneeze. I realize even beauty is dangerous, and nowhere is safe, as the wind blows more pollen toward my face.

"Lying"

It isn't the way you touch me; it's the way you don't touch me
gently with your fingertips gliding, the backs of your hands
smoothing skin over skin over skin, nerves tingling, desire rough
and new. It's obvious: I'm lying. It's the way you touch me; it's
the way you don't remember how sensitive I am, remember the
way my joints ache so suddenly, how often I call for you to
rescue me from the hallway, carry me to bed, stop groping my
tits, rough and greedy, pinching and squeezing, then right for the
clit, raw and hidden, exposed to harsh air, skin over skin over
skin, nerves burning, panic rough and familiar. It's obvious.

"Prolapse"

A fissure of sunshine through trees and clouds scatters lines
across my face, warm wind fraying my ravaged hair. 83 minutes
of exercise, 522 calories burned, 2 more hours to stand. I walk
toward dinner—my treat, I say to myself: heirloom tomatoes
grazing a whipped goat cheese and pesto mousse, strawberries
over Bibb lettuce, a sparkling rhubarb basil soda teasing my
tongue: a rich woman's feast. A quiet house in the wealthy part
of town. A wealth of discomfort no matter the chair; soft tissue
pushing beyond its limits, bulging, falling. Thirty-two years and
not a single one unmarred by a body never meant to survive—
not if ever untended. Maple and almonds blend with mint and
chicken. A cat groans in restful sleep. An unbearable sadness
settles in for the long night of despair, of wondering what might
happen next.

"The Absence of It"

Shadows frighten me, lately. Shadows of my own body that I
actively make: my body floating across the top of the chair until
the whole of it sits in darkness, my fingers cascading through a
bright portal of light slashed across the cherry wood of the
hallway floor like a warning.

When I realize it was me, should I feel better? I don't. I feel
worse.

I pull at the skin on my lips until I taste blood, no matter how
many times I tell myself I'll stop. When it grows back in small
sheets, the edges lift up again, some sheer kind of scab, and I feel
them with my tongue, on my other lip, on his—

I can't stand it.

I can't stand the thought of him not being able to stand it.

I can't stand the way my lips look on camera, mottled mauve on
pale skin. There's either blood or the reminder of blood, but
never the absence of it.

I wonder how long I would have to bleed to get there: the
absence of it.

"Release"

This is what you need to stretch his voice says, but his fingers
say it louder. He pushes to his left, deep inside me: the vice-like
sling around my organs.

This is what you need to stretch his fingers say, but his voice asks
if it hurts, and when I say no, we're both surprised—the
fluttering, constricting, lack of response.

This is what you need to stretch his fingers say, and then the
muscle gives like a coiled rubber band, releasing, warming—
open, relaxed, malleable.

That is what you need to stretch his voice says, then he asked if I
had control, and when I say no, we're not surprised—the pain,
the adhesions, the excisions of tissue, organ.

This is what you need to stretch his voice says, pointing to a
woman's pelvis, showing me the muscle that I cannot stretch
myself, that I cannot reach myself, that I cannot change.

"Binge"

Trails of foil—crumpled squares, balls—
tucked under layers of refuse, of paper towel
in tissues within tissues
from one treat, two, six, ten,
gooey fingers quickly rinsed, my mouth
thick with evidence,
insatiable,
my teeth rotting, sharp holes
catch my tongue, blood dribbles into the
lack of sugar, until
more foil finds my fingers, my stomach
wrenching at the thought of
more, at the thought of
less, at the thought of
you, finding
trails of foil

"Leigh Chadwick Pt. 4"

I learned that a bee sting can feel good if you squint just right. I learned that no sound will ever sound as good as the sounds that remind me of what never existed. I learned that something good is never just something good, and when they say no good deed goes unpunished, they mean happiness isn't real, whatever that is. I learned that a vagina is a curse, and nothing will ever feel better than the idea of something that can't happen. I learned how not to carry his shortcomings. I learned the key to baking: throw out the mirror. I learned that nothing I want will ever matter if I can't tell you about the flutter of my heart and the weakness in my legs—if you're not there to hold me up. I learned that you won't be there to hold me up.

"Thoughts Between Making Lunch and Meetings and Throwing Clothes in the Dryer"

I wish
you knew
how often
I wish
you knew
I wish
I could tell you
so much more.

"Leigh Chadwick Pt. 7"

I learned that writing letters in my head doesn't quiet the noise. Instead, I repeat the words over and over until I crumple a soft taco tortilla and smash it on the ground, imagining shards of dough scattering across the whole of Brookline. I learned that scribbling thoughts on scraps of paper and crumpling them into full paper bags stuffed with crushed cans and broken-down cardboard boxes does just about the same. I thought about lighting them on fire, but I learned I don't like to be conspicuous. I prefer not to be—at all. I learned that I can write a whole set of words on a postcard, even your address, burned into my selectively photographic memory, and fold the postcard haphazardly in half and stuff it into a recycling bin on Beacon Street, and I'll still wonder if, somehow, without any postage, no longer recognizable, it might make its way to you. I learned that the words will repeat day after day

after day after day after day after day after day after day after day
after day after day after day after day after day after day after day
after day after day after day after day after day after day after day
after day after day after day after day after day after day after day
after day after day after day after day after day after day after day
after day after day after day after day after day after day after day
after day after day after day after day after day after day after day
after day after day after day after day after day after day after day
after day after day after day after day after day after day after day
after day after day after day after day after day after day after day
after day after day after day after day after day after day after day
after day after day after day after day after day after day after day
after day after day after day after day after day after day after day
after day after day after day after day and still

"The Moment Between"

Sometimes, I wish I would turn a corner and you'd be there, standing, looking around, lost. Looking for me. Sometimes I think I could fall in love with just about anyone, given enough time. Sometimes I think about the gravitational pull between two people and how it's different from other pulls, different from other people, and why is that? And is there anything I can do to change it? Can I make it go away? Can I make it stop? Will it ever stop? Will I ever stop waiting for you? Sometimes, I think about the first time, coming around a corner, and the look on your face, and I know I knew it then. Sometimes—no, always, I miss the moment between knowing and what comes next.

"Grocery Shopping"

I sit in the sun like I have so many times and can't
enjoy the warmth on my face, the pain
claws too deep within my bowels, every organ screams,
Hear me, please, I'm begging, and I hear them, but I think,
There's nothing I can do.

I sit in the sun with the same song on
repeat—four, twelve, thirty-two times, she sings,
I never forgot; I've always been yours, and every organ
screams, *Hear me, please, I'm begging*, and you don't
hear them, but I think,
There's nothing you could do.

I sit in the sun, temperate rays generating
burns, aches like the many years gone by—3, 7, 8, the years to
come, inevitable, and every organ screams,
Hear me, please, I'm begging, and I tell them that I'll never
forget, but all else within me screams, *Forget.*

IV

"Autism Stanza 1"

A day begins the way a day begins: alarm ignored, silk blocking
light not blocked by other fabric. A day begins the way most
days begin: late, a rush to wake and locate myself, a crumple to
the floor on unsteady legs, frozen by the choices I give myself,
driven by obsession: too many clothes from which to choose,
paralyzed as promised moments tick by. A day begins the way
most days begin: drag a brush through blown-out hair meant to
last all week because I cannot hold a blow dryer for very long,
powder brushed over a pale face that hasn't seen sun in days—I
stopped counting. A day begins the way a day begins: in best
attempts gone untended, intentions unmoored because it isn't
possible to moor a boat made of papier-mâché.

"Autism Stanza 2"

A day becomes what a day becomes: pills before meals before other pills, timed and planned and counted, measured and measured again. A day becomes a series of decisions, guided and unguided, on good days measured and measured again, predictable and welcome, conversations scripted and mostly parsed. A bad day becomes a series of decisions, wholly unguided, unclear and unwelcome and unplanned, noise undeciphered and grating. A bad day becomes a series of decisions that become too much, like where to put one foot after the other, which direction to look, how many breaths I should take and whether or not it's okay to touch the things I know I own. A day becomes paralysis, a stomach flipped inside out, a skin all wrong. A day becomes a pill after a pill, then another pill, a hideout in a room where I can't find me, where I can leave my skin, maybe just for a moment.

"Autism Stanza 3"

A day becomes a night like other nights: my old skin, hanging in
the back room, and I wander into the rooms, alone and uncaring.
A night becomes a night: touch on new skin in all the right
places, liquid food that soothes and burns the way I wish all
things would burn. A night ends like all the other nights: pills
followed by pills followed by dreams of other lives, of other *mes*
with other skins and other days that become something else
entirely that I will never know.

"Leigh Chadwick Pt. 9"

I learned that no amount of preparation is enough when parts of
you have cancer or you're missing a lung. I learned that not
going to sleep on time might mean you feel like that guy in that
movie who has the ghost on his back the whole time. I learned
that sending a simple text can drain my energy, and that the way
I *feel* in a day can be stretched, clumped, kneaded, rolled out, cut
into shapes, and baked to look like a storybook but the *feel* part
doesn't change. I learned that the way I feel about most things is
limited, and that others don't understand when I try to explain. I
stopped trying to explain. I learned to live without validation and
that a moment is just a moment—it will pass, and so will we, a
blip on the calendar of the universe, barely a memory.

"Here's Another Poem"

Sometimes, I wonder about life with children,
but then I open my eyes.

"Leigh Chadwick Pt. 5"

I learned that no choice will ever feel quite right. I learned that everything is a series of reactions, and one wrong step might put you smack in the middle of a disastrous path. I learned that even a right step can't make any promises, and people will let you down long before they do anything that makes you smile, and by then you might be too far beneath the ground to remember why a smile matters. I learned that answers are the rarest of all currency, out of print before humankind blipped into existence, and most people have forgotten how to find them. I learned that even though I stopped eating wheat, onions, beans, apples, nectarines, garlic, and dairy, I still felt sick all the time, so what's the point? I learned that I have to make my own point, but I forgot how, so I stopped trying.

"The Pit Poem (Remix)"

Up out of the ground, out of nothing, a bottomless black pit
looms and consumes and swallows me whole. Inside the pit, I
can't see anything. I'm not sure where *a thing* begins and my
body ends. I wonder if a bottomless black pit can ever develop a
bottom, or if something molded can be salvaged or if it's always
actually tainted, or if when you break someone's heart, do the
cats feel it, too? Sometimes, I think I can still see the light, but
other times I know I've been falling for so long, I don't know
which way is up.

"Bone Conduction"

A vacuum starts in the foyer just *there* at 6:44 p.m. and drowns out the sound of *Suspiria*, so you pause and wait for it to stop.

In electric silence, a sadness sets in, a bone-deep weight against which you're helpless, so you sit and wait for it to pass.

A vacuum stops at 6:47 p.m., but sadness continues, an ache in your chest, physical, gnawing.

Two minutes of almost-silence pass slowly, drawn out, and still you wait, still the sadness deepens.

A vacuum starts at 6:49 p.m., and the ache in your chest ebbs and flows with the dance of the machine, this way and that, imagined lines on old carpet, sucking dust and decay.

Your bones pulse to the rhythm of your aching chest, and you know that waiting is pointless.

"The Gravity of Sadness (Remix)"

I wonder if love is ever actually love or if it's just pretending to
want to eat dinner together. I wonder if apple juice molds when
no one is looking, or if I would hear the shatter of my windshield
if I suddenly pulled the emergency brake as I headed, during
rush hour, eastbound on I-90. I wonder, *Would he still put the car
away if all the parking spots became grass?* Someone tells me,
*There are more than a few of us for whom life is an ache and a
long red glare over the horizon.* I ask her, *Will you tell your
daughter about the gravity of sadness, or will you hope she never
needs to know?* She collects a single tear in a vial and mails it to
2053. 2053 doesn't mail anything back. 2053 is an asshole. She
calls 2047 and says, *Can you believe 2053?* And 2047 says, *I
know, but it'll never be anything worth remembering.*
Somewhere, a rainbow forgets the color red. Somewhere, the
wind goes purple. Somewhere, ginger forgets how to burn, and
you turn pale.

"Leigh Chadwick Pt. 6"
—for K

I learned that when other people say time is a flat circle, they're joking around, having a bit of fun. They don't mean it the way I do—that everything repeats because it's all happening again and for the first time and the twentieth time all at once, that we can never understand the full meaning of time, a word we invented to name a concept that even the smartest can't nail down. I learned that some biological part of me will always want a baby, and that she'll sneak into my dreams and try to change my mind, even though I am an unwoman. I learned and relearned that stress can make me violently ill and that one single friend who understands can be the difference between life and death. I learned that if I choose life—because it is always a choice that requires making —I have to choose it every day. And the next day. And again. And again. I learned that the choice never stays made, no matter how set it might feel. I learned that tomorrow, everything will be different and the same and new and old and right and wrong all over again, because time is a flat circle.

"Someone Else's Timeline"

When she gives me the shiny pink trench coat, I don't throw it
out, and she doesn't spin into a fit of rage. When she walks into a
room, it fills with light and warmth, and I don't feel my chest
close in on itself like a cage tightened around my adrenal glands.
When she goes for a trip one weekend to see a friend, we don't
spend hours talking about the lies and the time she carved her
arm with a hunting knife and threatened suicide if he said
anything, or the time she climbed, naked, onto the roof at 3 a.m.
and threatened to jump. She doesn't call and ask him to come
halfway down Tiger Mountain to get all the jewelry because *no
one deserves a windfall from this.* We don't realize she's hacked
every account and has every password, taking photographs over
shoulders at opportune moments Christmas Eve, reading private
messages and tracking money spent. She doesn't make up stories
about awful things I never did, but instead we share and tell
secrets and laugh together. He doesn't cave when she asks to
come back, and I don't have to remind him that I can't live there
if she does, because she never needed to leave in the first place. I
don't find myself homeless after losing two homes to abusive
stepparents and eventually a third to fire. In someone else's
timeline, she's at my wedding, dabbing away the tears she can't
stop from welling, all but handing me away herself. And then
when the cancer gets bad, I don't have to beg to help them, to be
there; I don't write letters and send emails and text and call and
plead for some sort of resolution because I'm already with her,
holding her hand. And when she decides to go, she says
goodbye, that she loves me, that I was her daughter. In someone
else's timeline, she saw a doctor sooner because she allowed
herself to trust a stranger, and she'd be the first one reading
every line I wrote, the first one texting, earlier than I'd ever
wake, that I couldn't possibly make her prouder. And in that
someone else's timeline, that would be enough.

"Leigh Chadwick Pt. 8"

I learned that when someone dies, the only people who care are the people worth caring about. I learned that death can happen so suddenly and not suddenly enough, and that, when it does, it's never convenient, except maybe for the person who does the dying, because maybe they'd had enough of living. I learned that I'm not afraid of dying, but I am afraid of dying before you know, really know, what it all meant to me. I learned that a grown man will prioritize work over saying goodbye to someone he loves because, for years, he hasn't been allowed to be human. I learned that allowing someone to be human might bring them to tears, and that tears are contagious, and that it doesn't feel all that bad, but it doesn't feel good. I learned that I wish we could all be more honest, but honesty doesn't stop death, and it sure as fuck doesn't stop inhumanity. I learned that, sometimes, I simply can't fix it, and that feels worse than anything.

"What If"

What if, when I get on the plane to go to Chicago, it goes to
Chicago, but then I board another plane, any plane, and I go
somewhere different, and no one from this "life" ever hears from
me again, and I become someone else—would I be more or less
myself? What if I stopped taking all the pills and became
someone else—would I be less or more myself? I know these are
things we all wonder, we who take the pills. What if, one
Saturday morning, when I have no sense of reality, I slash my
arms open and out spills something black and thick and dark, and
the lights flicker and stop, and I realize: I am not awake; I have
never been awake; this isn't even me? What if, instead of
pretending to be happy, instead of taking the pills, I stop, and one
Saturday morning, I strip naked and run through the streets
because no one can really see me anyway, and even if they
could, would they care? What if, one Saturday morning, I cease
to speak, and I never make another sound? What if this meaning
and purpose we seek is something we will never find, so striving
for adequacy is asinine in the least, absurd at most? What if I am
nothing? What if, even then, I still love you, and you will never
even know?

"Leigh Chadwick Pt. 11"

I learned that I can kiss my husband goodbye—twice—robed in
pink-and-white toile that grazes the gleaming hardwood as I
close and lock the creaky door behind him, my new wildflower-
pink slippers on my feet, then sit on the electric reclining sofa
and press the button to lean back, almost flat, head supported by
a separate tilting function, two gleaming twin TVs and gaming
consoles straight ahead in front of hardwood-paneled walls and
perfect lighting in this brownstone walkup, and still, when I relax
my gaze to where the wood meets the eggshell wall and release
the muscles in my body—as close as I can get, which is far—so
that I am still in the quiet of a sleepy, expensive apartment, the
first image in my mind is of a razor, dragging ragged across my
skin, catching because I pull wildly from wrist to elbow, opening
vein after vein until blood pours from within—what blood I have
left after the seventeen recent draws—to dye the toile burgundy
and red, a change of scenery without leaving my seat, a new me,
born in death, left finally in peace. I learned that years, pills,
therapy, love—secret and not—cats, words, and hope can't take
this image from my mind, and that sadness is in my genetic code,
and it will follow me all my life. I learned that even for my
father, happy things are sad. I learned that the real tragedy is
pretending to be someone else, something else, some way else,
because all I can be is me, and all I can do is let the image be a
vision, nothing more, nothing less. I learned to let that be
enough.

"The Stillness of Time (Remix)"

I think about the effort it takes to walk from the living room to
the kitchen, to twist my mouth into one expression after another.
I ask, *If energy cannot be created or destroyed, will I run out
before I can ever smile at my wrinkles in the mirror?* I think
probably not. I can see the wrinkles already. I ask her, *Are
wrinkles good or bad?* She says, *Yes.* That's enough for now. She
catches the sun in a jar and puts the jar in a box she hides
underneath her bed. She says, *Not yet.* She says, *Hold on for one
more morning.* She says, *Let the sun bloom into a moment of
stillness*

Epilogue

"Leigh Chadwick Pt. X"

I learned that things that bore me from day to day take on new meaning when I almost die: the cat calling for me at midnight, incessantly, restless alone; the beauty of a messy kitchen only half-cleaned from a dinner only half-enjoyed but prepared with such passion: parsley, garlic, leeks in one corner of the floor, crushed cashew strewn about; the silence of sitting in a chair with nothing but my water and time. Precious time. I learned that I will never get enough of time—I gulp it, breathe it in, lust for more the second it slips by. I learned that some shame stays, but other shame whisps away like particles from a sneeze caught in a draft. I learned that I am grateful for this messy, difficult, deceitfully complex life I've built around me, and for the hand that keeps mine steady, even when the burden is too much. I have learned that it's often better to focus on the things I offer: mediocre dinners done far too late, pill boxes refilled, a cold body to counter his warmth, and time—so much time. I have learned to let that be enough.

Acknowledgements

A solo debut, whether poetry or prose, is often hard fought and sorely achieved, and mine is no exception. Thank you to Jeff for the constant support and for believing in my words. Thank you to the journals that previously published pieces or versions of pieces featured in this collection: *Salamander Magazine, Autofocus Lit, Stanchion Zine, HAD, Queerlings, trampset, Olney Magazine, No Contact Mag, Rejection Letters, Scrawl Place, Drunk Monkeys, mac(ro)mic, Hellebore Review, Papeachu Press*. Three poems were taken and remixed from original forms in *Too Much Tongue*, a collaborative collection written with Leigh Chadwick (Autofocus Books, 2022). Thank you to the friends who lent unyielding encouragement—Barlow, Danny, Jeffrey, Hassan, Dorian, Ashby, and my team at work. Thank you to Jay for being like a brother and always lifting me up. Thank you to Barlow, Micah, Lauren, GennaRose, Exodus, and Leigh for lending your words, in different ways, to this collection. Thank you to Kris for being a rock among shifting ground, understanding on a cellular level what others cannot. Your friendship is a gift to me. Thank you to Jaime for your keen eye and tender heart. Thank you to the bands, shows, movies, and novels providing the soundtrack to my life and writing: *Persuasion, Last Night, Wicker Park*, Stars, Brand New, The Fray, Sufjan Stevens, *One Tree Hill*, Nine Inch Nails.

Above all, thank you, again, to Leigh—my writing partner, my editor, my friend, my accomplice, my sounding board. Without you, my writing would be wholly different, and my life would be a lot more boring. I will always miss you.

About the Author

In addition to *We Don't Know That This Is* Temporary, Adrienne Marie Barrios is co-author of the poetry collection *Too Much Tongue* (Autofocus, 2022), written with Leigh Chadwick.

She is co-editor-in-chief of *Reservoir Road Literary Review* and editor-in-chief of *CLOVES Literary*. She Her work—poetry, creative nonfiction, and fiction—has appeared in numerous literary journals. She edits award-winning novels, poetry collections, short stories, and anthologies.

Adrienne is autistic and has ADHD and struggles daily with chronic illnesses and disability. Many days, she struggles simply to exist, but the pain borne of those days gives way to a creativity she isn't sure she would've found otherwise. She owes much of her continued survival to her husband, their four cats, and her few close friends who know what it means to persevere.

ALSO AVAILABLE FROM STANCHION BOOKS

The Woman's Part by Jo Gaword

The House of Skin by Karina Lickorish Quinn

Where We Set Our Easel by Mandira Paanaik

Irregulars by Kerry Trautman

It Skips A GeneraIon by Alison Lubar

Ghost Mom by T Guzman

The Unaccounted for Circles of Hell by Lynne Schmidt

UNTENABLE MYSTIC CHARM by travis l. tate

Thoughts I Lost in the Laundry by Leia Butler

My Dungeon Love Affair by Stephanie Parent

Learn more at StanchionZine.com

9 798892 926836